Bhagavad-gita for Children

Our Most Dear Friend

written and illustrated by
Vishaka

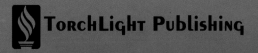

For their support, encouragement, and advice, many
thanks to Robert A., John, and Amrita Griesser,
Alister and Victoria Taylor, Bert and Morissa Dougherty,
Bob and Peggy Edell, Yamaraja Das, and Kim Arnold.

Printed in Hong Kong.
Published simultaneously in the United States of America,
Canada, Brazil, and Croatia by Torchlight Publishing.

Library of Congress Cataloging-in-Publication Data
Vishaka, 1950-
    Our Most Dear Friend : Bhagavad-gita for children / Vishaka.
        p.   cm.
    Summary : Presents the essence of the scripture that forms the basis of India's
spiritual culture and which is revered by 850 million people world-wide.
    ISBN: #1-887089-04-7 (hc) : $14.95 ($21.50 Can.)
    I. Bhagavadgita.   English.   II. Title.   95-46070
BL 1138.64.E5   1996   CIP
294.5 ' 924--dc20   AC

The montages in this book were created from black-and-white
handtinted photographs by the author.

Readers interested in the subject matter of this book are invited
to correspond with the author at:
Torchlight Publishing
P.O. Box 177,
Badger,
CA 93603 USA
or phone: (209) 337-2200.

To His Divine Grace
A.C. Bhaktivedanta Swami Prabhupada
who gave us *Bhagavad-gita As It Is*
and who is our ever well-wisher.

Once, long, long ago in India, many thousands of warriors gathered at Kurukshetra, a holy place of pilgrimage. Here they would fight a great battle to decide whether the noble Pandava brothers or the evil-minded Kaurava brothers would rule the land.

War horses, elephants, chariots, armor, bows and arrows, swords, shields, spears, and maces were ready. Within moments a terrible war would begin.

Then Arjuna, one of the Pandava brothers and an expert archer, asked his chariot driver, Lord Krishna, to drive their chariot between the two huge armies. Upon seeing friends and relatives on the enemy side, Arjuna became confused about whether or not he should fight.

Humbly, Arjuna turned to Lord Krishna for guidance.

At this point, the Supreme Lord, Krishna — playing the role of a chariot driver — began to instruct His devotee and friend Arjuna. And by instructing Arjuna, He also instructed all people. The Lord's sweet, immortal words are the *Bhagavad-gita*, the song of God.

Lord Krishna first explained that there is a difference between your body and you, a tiny soul within your body. Your body was born and will die, but you, a soul, were never born and will never die. The soul lives forever and the soul is the real self.

Within every living thing there is a soul. The soul gives life to flowers, plants, and trees, to insects, birds, fish, and animals.

And it is the soul that gives life to your body.

Lord Krishna continued, "Your body passed from childhood to youth and will one day become old. But the soul within your body is not affected by these changes.

"When you die the soul gives up the body to enter another one, just as you give up an old coat to put on a new one.

"As the sun fills the sky with sunlight, so the soul fills the body with consciousness.

"The soul cannot be hurt or killed — not by fire, weapons, the wind or anything else. Only the body can be hurt or killed."

"When you understand the soul, you will be joyful and will never forget your higher, spiritual nature. Even if great trouble comes, you will not be disturbed.

"When you understand the soul you will see that all living beings are part of Me, the Supreme Spirit — God. You will see that they are My children and are spiritually equal. And you will be kind to all living beings, knowing that they are all dear to Me."

Lord Krishna said to Arjuna,
"As the sun lights everything in
the daytime, so when someone
loves and serves Me, he can
understand everything easily.

"For a person who is devoted
to Me, I am always with him
and he is always with Me.
Such a person is not lazy or
selfish and works to please Me.

"Know Me as your final goal,
as the Lord of everything, and
as the well-wisher of everyone.
With this knowledge be
peaceful and happy."

Arjuna asked, "But what happens to a person who tries to be devoted to You for some time and then stops? Is he like a wind-blown cloud with no position in either the material or the spiritual world?"

"My friend," Lord Krishna answered, "one who does good is never overcome by evil. In his next birth such a person will have the chance to begin his devotional service to Me again."

Then Arjuna said, "I totally accept all You have told me. O Lord of the universe, please tell me of Your powers and how I should think of You. Tell me of Your might and glory, for I never tire of hearing Your sweet words."

Lord Krishna said, "Yes, I will tell you of My powers, but only some of them, for they are endless. When you see or hear of anything great in this world, remember Me. All beautiful, glorious, and mighty creations are only a spark of My splendor.

"I am the life of all that lives, the original seed of all life. I am the intelligence of the intelligent. And I am the strength of all powerful men.

"I am seated next to the soul in the heart of every creature. I am the light of the sun and the moon, and the heat in fire. I am the taste of water, I am the ocean, I am unending time, and of seasons I am flower-bearing spring. I am victory, adventure, ability and wisdom.

"I am sound. And of secrets, I am silence."

Lord Krishna continued, "I know everything that happened in the past, all that is happening at present, and all that is yet to come.

"Everything happens by My rule — even the blades of grass move by My desire.

"Everything comes from Me. I am the source of the material and spiritual worlds.

"Everything rests upon Me just as pearls rest on a thread.

"There is no truth above Me.

"And I am your most dear friend."

"The world becomes joyful upon hearing Your name. Godly people offer You their worship, but ungodly people are afraid and run away from You.

"Whatever You do is good for everyone. You are to be worshiped by every living being. I offer You my respect and my love."

Arjuna said, "O Krishna, You are the Supreme Lord. All the great sages have said this, and now You Yourself are saying it to me.

"My dear Arjuna," the Lord said, "always think of Me and serve Me with love. Then you will understand Me.

"When your service to Me never stops and is done only for My pleasure, and when you are friendly to every living being, I will lead you from this world of birth and death.

"I will bring you to My home, where there is no birth, no death, and no unhappiness. There you will enjoy life forever."

"Arjuna," the Lord finally said, "I want you to fight this war so that you and your good brothers will become the rulers of this land. But, after hearing what I have said, you may do whatever you wish."

"My dear Krishna," Arjuna said, "I am no longer confused or sad, and I am ready to act as You desire."

Wherever there is Krishna, the Supreme Lord, and Arjuna, the supreme archer, there will also be wealth, power, goodness, and . . . victory!

After eighteen days of fierce fighting, the Pandava brothers won the war and became the rightful rulers. Under their leadership, the people became peaceful, prosperous, and happy.

Afterword

In the introduction to his *Bhagavad-gita As It Is*, His Divine Grace A. C. Bhaktivedanta Swami Prabhupada writes, ". . . Recently an American lady asked me to recommend an English translation of *Bhagavad-gita*. Of course in America there are so many editions of *Bhagavad-gita* available in English, but as far as I have seen, not only in America but also in India, none of them can be strictly said to be authoritative because in almost every one of them the commentator has expressed his own opinions without touching the spirit of *Bhagavad-gita* as it is.

"The spirit of *Bhagavad-gita* is mentioned in *Bhagavad-gita* itself. It is just like this: If we want to take a particular medicine, then we have to follow the directions written on the label. We cannot take the medicine according to our own whim or the direction of a friend. It must be taken according to the directions on the label or the directions given by a physician. Similarly, *Bhagavad-gita* should be taken or accepted as it is directed by the speaker himself. The speaker of *Bhagavad-gita* is Lord Sri Krishna. He is mentioned on every page of *Bhagavad-gita* as the Supreme Personality of Godhead, Bhagavan. . ."

Srila Prabhupada's complete *Bhagavad-gita*, with the original Sanskrit text, Roman transliterations, English equivalents, translation, and elaborate purports is available from The Bhaktivedanta Book Trust at:

P.O. Box 324   P.O. Box 262   3764 Watseka Ave.
Borehamwood, Herts.   Botany, N.S.W.   Los Angeles
WD6 1NB, U.K.   2019, Australia   CA 90034, USA.

This present version of *Bhagavad-gita* is an attempt to bring Srila Prabhupada's mood and message to children.

Vishaka
January, 1996